FASTING

by

a Friend of Medjugorje

See page 136 for Pricing.
For additional copies write: **Caritas of Birmingham**
100 Our Lady Queen of Peace Drive
Sterrett, AL 35147 USA
Call 205-672-2000 press ext. 315 (24 hours a day)

Published with permission from SJP Lic. COB.

Copyright © 2022, SJP.	Copyright © 2015, SJP.	Copyright © 2008, SJP.	Copyright © 2001, SJP.
Copyright © 2020, SJP.	Copyright © 2014, SJP.	Copyright © 2007, SJP.	Copyright © 1999, SJP.
Copyright © 2019, SJP.	Copyright © 2013, SJP.	Copyright © 2006, SJP.	Copyright © 1998, SJP.
Copyright © 2018, SJP.	Copyright © 2011, SJP.	Copyright © 2004, SJP.	Copyright © 1997, SJP.
Copyright © 2017, SJP.	Copyright © 2010, SJP.	Copyright © 2003, SJP.	
Copyright © 2016, SJP.	Copyright © 2009, SJP.	Copyright © 2002, SJP.	

ISBN: 978-1-878909-37-4

©SJP International Copyright. All rights reserved including international rights. No part of this short book may be reproduced or transmitted in any form or by any means, electronic or mechanical, including photocopying, recording, or by any information storage or retrieval system, without permission in writing from Caritas who is licensed to use the material. Caritas of Birmingham, 100 Our Lady Queen of Peace Drive, Sterrett, Alabama 35147 USA. None of the mailing lists of Caritas or its entities, including electronic mailing lists, etc., are for sale, nor is permission given to use them in anyway, by anyone. There are no exceptions. All civil, criminal, interstate, and international violations of law apply.

Table of Contents

5	ABOUT THE AUTHOR
9	STORY IN BRIEF

FASTING
11 INTRODUCTION

PART ONE
14 SIXTY FACTS OUR LADY TELLS US ABOUT FASTING.

PART TWO
24 WHAT AMAZING THINGS WILL FASTING DO? WHAT WILL CHANGE?

PART THREE
45 A FRIEND OF MEDJUGORJE ANSWERS THE MOST ASKED QUESTIONS ABOUT FASTING.

PART FOUR
69 HOW TO RADICALLY INCREASE YOUR INTERMITTENT FASTING SUCCESS

74	FASTING IS GOOD FOR YOUR HEART, BRAIN AND WAISTLINE
78	THE 5:2 INTERMITTENT FASTING PLAN
81	MY PERSONAL RECOMMENDATIONS (DR. MERCOLA) [AND INSULIN PROBLEMS]
84	WHO SHOULD USE EXTRA CAUTION WHEN FASTING, OR AVOID IT ALTOGETHER?

PART FIVE

92	COLAFRANCESCO'S ITALIAN BREAD RECIPE
95	THE RICHNESS OF A BREAD PAN
99	COLAFRANCESCO'S ITALIAN BREAD RECIPE
127	WANT MORE THAN JUST SLICED BREAD?
129	FASTING: A STRONG FOUNDATION

About the Witness

Many who will read these books have been following the writings of a Friend of Medjugorje for years. His original and unique insights into the important events of our day have won credence in hundreds of thousands of hearts around the world, with those affecting others, thereby, touching into the millions. His moral courage in the face of so many leaders caving in to the pressures of a politically correct world is not only refreshing, but, according to tens of thousands of written testimonies over 35 years, has helped to strengthen deeply those who desire to live the fullness of their Christian faith. His insights have repeatedly proven prophetic, having their source in the apparitions of the Virgin Mary in Medjugorje. Deeply and personally influenced by the events surrounding Medjugorje, he gave himself to the prayerful application of the words of the Virgin Mary into his life. He has spoken all over the world on Our Lady's messages and how to put them into everyday life. He came to understand that Our Lady was sent by God to speak to mankind in this time because the dangers man is facing are on a scale unlike any the world has ever known since Noah and the flood. He is not an author. He is a witness of what Our Lady has shown him to testify to—first, by his life—secondly, through the written word. He is not one looking in from the outside regarding Medjugorje, but one who is close to the events—many times, right in the middle of the events about which he has written.

Originally writing to only a few individuals in 1987, readership has grown well into the millions in the United States and in over 130 foreign countries, who follow the spiritual insights and direction given through these writings.

When asked why he signs only as "a Friend of Medjugorje," he stated:

"I have never had an ambition or desire to write. I do so only because God has shown me, through prayer, that He desires this of me. So from the beginning, when I was writing to only a few people, I prayed to God and promised I would not sign anything; that the writings would have to carry themselves and not

be built on a personality. I prayed that if it was God's desire for these writings to be inspired and known, then He could do it by His Will and grace and that my will be abandoned to it.

"The Father has made these writings known and continues to spread them to the ends of the earth. These were Our Lord's last words before ascending: ***'Be a witness to the ends of the earth.'*** *These writings give testimony to that desire of Our Lord, to be a witness with one's life. It is not important to be known. It is important to do God's Will."*

For those who require "ownership" of these writings by the 'witness' in seeing his name printed on this work in order to give it more credibility, we, Caritas of Birmingham and the Community of Caritas, state that we cannot reconcile the fact that these writings are producing hundreds of thousands of conversions, and will easily be into the millions, through God's grace. His writings are requested worldwide from every corner of the earth. His witness and testimony, therefore, will not take credit for a work that, by proof of the impact these writings have to lead hearts to conversion, has been Spirit-inspired, with numbers increasing yearly, sweeping as a wave across the ocean. Indeed, in this case, crossing every ocean of the earth. Our Lady gave this Witness a direct message, through the Medjugorje visionary, Marija, and part of what Our Lady said to him was to **"…witness not with words but through humility…"** (Oct. 6, 1986) It is for this reason that he wishes to remain simply, "A Friend of Medjugorje."

In order to silence the voice of this witness, darkness has continually spewed out slanders to prevent souls from reading his convicting and life-changing writings. For if these writings were not so, darkness would ignore them or even lead people to them. But Jesus promised persecution to all those who follow Him, and the same will be to those who follow His Mother. *"If they persecuted me, they will also persecute you."* John 15:20

As a witness in real time of Our Lady's time on earth, his witness and writings will continue to speak—voicing Our Lady's Way to hundreds of millions not yet born—in the centuries to come.

— Caritas of Birmingham

Medjugorje
The Story in Brief

A VILLAGE SEES THE LIGHT is the title of a story which "Reader's Digest" published in February 1986. It was the first major news on a mass public scale that told of the Virgin Mary visiting the tiny village of Medjugorje, Bosnia-Hercegovina. At that time this village was populated by 400 families.

It was June 24, 1981, the Feast of John the Baptist, the proclaimer of the coming Messiah. In the evening, around 5:00 p.m., the Virgin Mary appeared to two young people, Mirjana Dragičević* and Ivanka Ivanković*. Around 6:40 p.m. the same day, Mirjana and Ivanka, along with four more young people, Milka Pavlović*, the little sister of Marija, Ivan Ivanković, Vicka Ivanković*, and Ivan Dragičević saw the Virgin Mary. The next day, June 25, 1981, along with Mirjana, Ivanka, Vicka and Ivan Dragičević, Marija Pavlović* and Jakov Čolo also saw the Virgin Mary, bringing the total to six visionaries. Milka Pavlović* and Ivan Ivanković only saw Our Lady once, on that first day. These six have become known as and remain "the visionaries."

These visionaries are not related to one another. Three of the six visionaries no longer see Our Lady on a

---
* Names at the time of the apparitions, they are now married with last names changed.

daily basis. As of September 2022, the Virgin is still appearing everyday to the remaining three visionaries; that's well over 17,588 apparitions. This count is each day for all the visionaries together in the apparitions. The visionaries have been separated for more years than together, which means the number is minimum 30 years × 3 visionaries who still see Our Lady daily being separated during apparition time.

The supernatural event has survived all efforts of the Communists to put a stop to it, many scientific studies, and even the condemnation by the local bishop; yet, the apparitions have survived, giving strong evidence that this is from God because nothing and no one has been able to stop it. For over 41 years, the apparitions have proved themselves over and over and now credibility is so favorable around the world that the burden of proof that this is authentic has shifted from those who believe to the burden of proof that it is not happening by those opposed to it. Those against the apparitions are being crushed by the fruits of Medjugorje — millions and millions of conversions which are so powerful that they are changing and will continue to change the whole face of the earth.

See **mej.com** for more information.
or **Medjugorje.com**

Fasting

Introduction

The word appears at least 100 times* in Our Lady's messages. It is a subject which does not necessarily bring about great excitement, yet many are interested in it. Over the years many have requested we write about it. Our Lady certainly holds it as a major part, a part of the very foundation of all of Her plans. And indeed it is: it is "fasting." We have learned many things from Our Lady about fasting through Her messages, one being its power. The magnificent lucifer, being the greatest creature next to God while in Heaven, had enormous power, but turned away from God. When he fell, he not only retained this great power, but also carried with him, to the side of darkness, his master intellect.

---

* This was originally written in 1997. A Friend of Medjugorje's writings often relate to the future, even prophetically, which becomes apparent in the present when one realizes the date it was originally written. As of March 2, 2022, Our Lady has mentioned fasting 193 times.
—The Community of Caritas

We cannot outsmart him or out power his mighty strength. Our Lady said on January 14, 1985:

> "**...satan is strong. He wishes with all his strength to destroy my plans...**"

We also have learned from Our Lady that while satan is possessed with every bad vice that can be imagined, laziness is not one of them. He is a very hard worker and is never caught sleeping. On the contrary, he watches constantly for you to drop your guard. Our Lady said on January 14, 1985:

> "**...he** (satan) **works very hard in the world. Be on your guard.**"

Only fools would think they could defeat satan or outwit him through their own strength. But what if we were told by Our Lady that She would give us a special gift, a power over satan's power; a strength to conquer not only this mighty beast but all his legions as well? How wonderful this would be.

How great this power must be to defeat so massive a power such as what satan holds.

While we are but weak creatures, by comparison, to these evil forces which are constantly on the prowl for us, we have a special strength, an armament, a weapon, coupled with prayer, which will conquer this evil power which Our Lady speaks of in this way.

> **"...Dear children, satan is lurking for each individual. Especially in everyday affairs, he wants to spread confusion among each one of you..."**
> September 4, 1986

Fasting is an armament, as Our Lady calls it. The weapon or "arm" in which to destroy satan's power in your life.

PART I

Sixty Facts Our Lady Tells Us About Fasting

FACTS ABOUT FASTING BROUGHT TO LIGHT IN MEDJUGORJE BY OUR LADY

1. **Fasting stops wars.** 7/21/82
2. **Fasting can suspend the laws of nature.** 7/21/82
3. **Fasting reduces punishments from God.** 11/6/82 **Fasting is an "arm," a weapon of significant power to defeat.** (Of which atomic power does not compare. Atomic power has not the strength to conquer satan.) 6/25/92

4. **Bread and water is the best fast.** 7/21/82

5. **Fasting, to be powerful, must be done with the heart.** 9/20/84

6. **Through fasting, the whole plan of Our Lady that God Himself planned for the world's salvation during this special time, will be achieved.** 9/26/85

7. **By giving our fasting to Our Lady, it "forces" satan not to be able to seduce us to evil and drives him away.** 9/4/86

8. **Fasting purifies our hearts from the sins of our past.** (Through Confession, sins of the past are forgiven, but healing from life-long vice or memories, which satan uses against us to lead us back into sin, requires purification). 12/4/86

9. **Fasting, coupled with prayer, will obtain everything you ask for** (the exception would be something illicit*). 10/29/83

---

*Illicit means not permitted; unlawful.

10. **Fasting sanctifies you to receive the Holy Spirit.** 11/4/83

11. **Humility is a fruit of fasting, when coupled with prayer.** 2/10/84

12. <u>**The present fasting in the Church is not adequate.**</u> **Our Lady desires this to change. She said** <u>**fasting has been forgotten in the last quarter of this century in the Catholic Church.**</u> May 1984

13. **Fasting is one element which keeps satan from conquering us. Faith and prayer are the other two.** 11/16/81

14. **We, in turn, are to conquer satan. The arms to do so are fasting, coupled with prayer.** 6/25/92

15. **satan is enraged against those who fast and convert.** 8/15/83

16. **Fasting for the sick can cure them, along with faith and prayer.** 11/26/81

17. **Fasting, along with prayer, was offered as a remedy by Our Lady to stop arguments among the Holy Priesthood.** 1/21/82

18. **Fasting will bring the Kingdom of God among us.** 3/14/84

19. **Fasting makes Our Lady happy.** 8/5/84

20. **Fasting will make prayer more vigorous.** 1/25/84

21. **Our Lady will make the maximum good come from our fast. She wants us to give our fasts to Her in which She "disposes of them" according to the Will of God.** 9/4/82

22. **Fasting, coupled with prayer, especially community prayer, will protect you from satan's aggression in destroying marriages, creating division among priests and will crush him in his plans for obsessions and murders in society today of which Our Lady says satan is responsible.** Before 12/26/82

23. **To obtain a grace from God, it is best you let no one know you are fasting.** 1/28/87

24. **We are to fast out of gratitude.** 9/20/84

25. **Fasting is to be <u>encouraged</u> to others.** 2/22/88

26. **Our Lady tells us to fast to prepare for the coming of Jesus!!** 11/25/96

27. **Fasting, coupled with renunciation, strengthens you, and your prayer will then be powerful enough to overcome your own will and discover God's Will.** 3/25/98

28. **Fasting is one–third of a foundation that will renew fervor in you of which Our Lady exposes in order that She will transform you so that you will find <u>true</u> peace.** (Prayer and conversion make up the other two-thirds.) 10/25/98

29. **Our Lady says you are "mine." Becoming "Hers," is achieved by fasting and prayer as Her witnesses.** 4/25/99

30. **The whole world is affected by you individually fasting and is on the brink of being renewed. Fasting is specifically requested by Our Lady so She can offer it to Her Son for a new Pentecost, a new Springtime in the Church which will affect all of creation.** 10/25/00

31. Fasting immunes one from the "fear" of evil. The one who fasts is not afraid of the future. Fasting, coupled with prayer, stops wars of unbelief and fear. 1/25/01

32. When man's heart is without peace, fasting, coupled with prayer, will cause it to visit his heart and be renewed in peace. 6/25/00

33. Fasting strengthens prayer and allows God to give you peace. 9/25/01

34. Peace is a precious gift from God in which, when you seek and fast for it, with prayer, you will receive the gift. 2/25/03

35. Fasting will enable you to see Jesus in each of your neighbors. Our Lady wants us to fast for this intention of Hers. 3/18/05

36. Novenas of fasting and renunciation will keep satan far from you and grace around you. 7/25/05

37. Fasting and prayer purifies our hearts to enable us to recognize and receive Jesus. 1/2/06

38. **Our Lady calls us to interior renunciation which will enable us to recognize** *the signs of the time in which we live.* **To more fully recognize the signs, fasting is necessary.** 3/18/06

39. **Fasting is a weapon in which you fight those obstacles which keep you from coming closer to Her Son.** 1/2/07

40. **The star that guides you through the spiritual life is fasting, coupled with prayer.** 3/2/07

41. **It is Our Lady's desire that your heart be purified by fasting.** 3/18/07

42. **Through fasting and prayer, you will be stronger in faith.** 3/25/07

43. **Fasting, coupled with prayer, purifies and gives you simple hearts. Our Lady says that only in the simplicity of your hearts is your salvation.** 9/2/07

44. **The human heart will choose good or evil to grow in the heart. Fasting ensures good will fruit in it.** 1/25/08

45. **Our Lady reveals fasting will help one to become conscious and carry out God's Will.** 10/25/08

46. **Our Lady tells us fasting will clear the way for Jesus to enter your heart and free you from the sense of guilt and everything from the past that burdens you and all that brought you to error.** 6/2/10

47. **Our Lady tells us that fasting gives us the strength to live God's love and be an example to those who do not know it.** 3/2/11

48. **Our Lady calls us to fast for Her intentions, for it is a protection from satan, who wants to destroy Her plans.** 8/25/11

49. **Our Lady asks us to fast because it is only in this way we will know how to witness Her Son in the right way.** 3/18/12

50. **Our Lady calls us to renew fasting to recognize that satan is cunning and attracts many hearts to sin and perdition.** 10/25/12

51. Our Lady tells us that through fasting, along with prayer and reconciliation, She will be able to lead us. 1/2/13

52. Our Lady tells us that fasting strengthens us so that we can live as the Heavenly Father would desire, and thereby bless those whom we meet. 5/2/13

53. Fasting, coupled with prayer, is the way to become cognizant of the Heavenly Father. 6/2/13

54. Our Lady tells us that through fasting, apostles will be '<u>born</u>' who will keep opening the gates of Heaven to all of Her children, apostles born for the task to bring these children to come to know the love of God. 7/2/13

55. Through fasting, we can learn to listen with the heart, submitting ourselves to reject everything that distances us from God's word. 9/2/13

56. When we fast, we will be able to recognize all that Our Lady is seeking of us. 12/2/13

57. **By fasting, we obtain from the Heavenly Father the cognition of what is natural and holy - Divine, retaining God's grace that descends upon us.** 2/2/14

58. **Every fast draws one closer, renewing the union with the Father and His children.** 4/2/14

59. **Fasting enables one to love God above everything.** 8/2/14

60. **Fasting will overcome many false truths that are being offered to you. Fasting cleanses the heart, fortified with prayer, penance and the Scriptures.** 1/2/15

PART II

What Amazing Things Will Fasting Do? What Will Change?

There is so much good that comes from fasting. It has a great deal to do with defeating satan, but it is God who does it. satan cannot do except that which God allows. Through fasting, we move God to bind satan. God is sensitive to hearts that deny their hunger because of love for Him, and so God reciprocates by granting grace to kill satan's plans or hold on us. Three things are necessary for God to do this:

1. **Prayer**
2. **Fasting**
3. **Surrendering and letting God Act**

Our Lady said on April 17, 1986:

"Pray. Fast. Let God act."

It is almost incomprehensible the power that is available to us. A power which all armaments, such as weapons, bombs, ships, missiles, aircraft, and troops from all the armies of the world combined together, now in the present, as well as all past history's armaments, does not equal to one person's fasting from the heart for one day. For all those things cannot move God to grant a request. Yet, one man with a pure fast from the heart, full of love, can move all of Heaven into action. It can boggle the mind to see all the world's medical technology, the best specialists in the world confront an incurable disease and be defeated, only to be outshined and confounded by a simple cure brought about by fasting and prayer.

How is it we are so privileged to be given such a profoundly wonderful gift? Fasting, if viewed as a burden, will gain you nothing. It is a gift to be allowed to do it, a gift given by our good God who then responds to it by answering our prayers. How gracious is our God to tell us, ***"I will give you a way when all else fails. I will accept it as payment if done from the heart and in return grant to you those 'needs in life' of which you request."***

But what if you do not have the strength to fast? Our Lady tells us:

April 17, 1986

"Pray...for the gift of fasting."

One man prepared for months in prayer knowing he would be in Medjugorje on his birthday. He had been praying for Our Lady to give him a gift of Her choosing. On April 24, 1988, he, with Marija, went to St. James choir loft for the apparition. Only Marija, Father Slavko, and he were present. During the apparition, he gave all his months of prayers to Our Lady with deep love for Her. He understood during the apparition that Our Lady gave him something, but he did not know what it was. However, over the course of the week, it became explicitly clear to him. He felt in the apparition the reception of two gifts. One was the ability of deep prayer and the second, that of fasting. Fasting became, from that time forward, a real desire. To this day, there is a grace within his heart that makes him deeply dissatisfied with himself if he does not or cannot fast because of certain events.

Our Lady has told us that love is a gift from God. God is the source of all good, so we can reason everything that is "good" comes from Him who is good. Since Our Lady tells us fasting is a gift, it, therefore, originates from Him who is good. Fasting cannot help but contain a great deal of good when performed from the heart. How does fasting affect us? There are several "good" fruits from fasting. One is it helps in giving us the ability to conquer fault and sin. Many in the world today are led to hell by their flesh. The flesh, in its cravings and desires for gluttony, sensuality, pleasure, comfort, etc., is in charge of most souls today. For the most part, in the present day, the soul, in its desires for purity and moderation, is dominated by the flesh and its senses. So much is offered in excess to the flesh today that without fasting, the flesh will always win when there is a struggle between the soul and the flesh. To follow the flesh is to lead to death, as well as loss of peace. To follow the spirit is to lead to life and peace. When a man follows the flesh and its desires, he is hostile to God and will not submit to God's law. The flesh cannot bend to God's will. Those who are into the flesh cannot please God. We, therefore, must become spirit. Whoever does not have the spirit of God dwelling in him does not belong to God. We are not to live according to the flesh, rather by our spirits. However, most do not do so. Rather than a soul leading the flesh, it is the flesh leading the soul. Sadly, many of those who live by the flesh are leading the soul directly to hell. Therefore, it can be said that if you live according to the flesh you will die eternally, but if you put your soul in charge and put to death deeds of the body you will live. If you are led by your soul, you are sons of God. St. Paul did a strange thing in Corinth. In the early Christian community, he turned over a man to satan to destroy his body so that he could save his spirit from the sin of incest. St. Paul says:

1 Corinthians 5:5

> ***"...you are to deliver this man to satan for the destruction of his flesh, so that his spirit may be saved on the day of the Lord."***

Perhaps the whole community of Corinth was praying for this man. God's answer was St.

Paul's action. How many family members or friends are prayed for, and God sends tribulation by satan's hand? Job was tried by satan though he was just. How much more are trials necessary for unjust souls in order to move them toward conversion? Volunteer fasting can save us a lot of misery and even health problems. Sin always brings unpeace; unpeace brings worry; worry can bring anger; anger can bring bitterness; bitterness, like acid, destroys the container that holds it. Sin destroys health. Fasting improves it. Purifying the soul brings peace. St. Paul's action of turning this man's flesh over to satan was to purify him of his sin and vice. God allows the same thing except in the exchange of fasting. It will not only save us, but also save us from many other things that may plague us that God may allow to get our attention. His love deems this in order to save us. Israel's history shows God purifying the nation repeatedly in order to draw it to Him. Yet, the sacrifice of fasting saved the city of Nineveh, which Jonah predicted

God had plans to destroy. The ways of God and His infinite love are clear for those who wish to understand it. Fasting has the same results of that action of St. Paul in that it kills inordinate desires and tendencies. God, the loving God He is, prefers us to voluntarily purify ourselves with fasting.

But what of the soul and flesh working together? Both the soul and the flesh cannot be in charge at the same time. There is a constant struggle to compromise between the two. Compromise means to make a shameful concession and to endanger, yet there is no room for compromise in the Christian life. The soul and the flesh are directly opposed to each other and will never be brought in harmony together without the loss of the soul, if it does not repent.

Galatians 5:17 states:

> ***"For the desires of the flesh are against the Spirit and the desires of***

the spirit are against the flesh for these are opposed to each other..."

It is why Our Lady is so strong about fasting. She wants the fruits of the flesh to die and the fruits of the spirit, of your soul, to live. The Bible tells us the fruits of the flesh are: fornication, impurity, licentiousness, idolatry, sorcery, enmity, strife, jealousy, anger, selfishness, dissension, lasciviousness, envy, drunkenness, carousing, etc...

The fruits of the spirit are love, joy, peace, patience, kindness, goodness, faithfulness, gentleness, and self-control. Jesus was crucified in His passion, and we are to crucify our passions.

Galatians 5:24

> *"And those who belong to Christ Jesus have crucified their flesh with its passions and desires."*

Our Lady's strong emphasis on fasting, if followed, will not only bring us individual peace but will usher in a world of peace. When a soul is in harmony with his God, there can be no storm within man, even though a storm may surround him. On the other hand, the flesh can be on fire with desire, all the while surrounded with calm.

When you decide to fast, immediately you are making a declaration of war. The good side inclined towards good—the soul, tells the side inclined towards bad—the flesh, *"Today you will come under my control, and I will make you good."* The flesh, of course, responds back by saying, *"No, you will be under my control."* The body certainly does not want this and will violently complain. The stomach will let you know it is very "upset" with your spirit's decision and, as the day or days of your fast progress, will do everything to let you know about it. The soul's answer, in order to win the battle, must be, *"NO! I will feed you when I am ready."* The stomach will go so far as to tell you, *"Feed me or I'll be a real headache for you,"* which indeed will tell the head to *"hurt for awhile"* in order to make the soul give in. But slowly, with a firm decision to fast, the flesh will calm down, its passions quelled and prayer invigorated. You will begin to experience deeper prayer, peace and purity.

The sense of joy your soul experiences because of its coming closer to God and growing in strength, will manifest itself in your heart. A good feeling will be within you, knowing the flesh is under control and tamed. The early Christians fasted on Wednesdays and Fridays. Our Lady has invited the same today, and two days a week on bread and water is sufficient in growing in strength to control the flesh. Fasting is to the soul as jogging is to the body. It exercises the soul, strengthening it to stand up to the flesh and dominate its passions to makes the flesh conform.

The more a jogger runs, the better shape he gets in. He becomes stronger and can run greater distances. A marathon runner may exercise for years, building up his capability to run non-stop for 26 miles or more. The human body builds its strength the more it is used. The soul is not without the same results. The more you fast, the stronger the spirit becomes. Fasting strengthens prayer; prayer strengthens fasting, feeding each other. Fasting serves to "jog the soul," giving it the ability to have a tremendous strength and to even reach sanctity, the real test or spiritual marathon.

Temptations will be deflected with greater ease because you will hear more clearly the promptings of your soul which receives greater graces because of your fasting. Your soul will then lead your flesh, and Heaven will be attentive to your prayer. This is the desire of Our Lady and the proper order. Unfortunately, it is completely reversed in today's society, and the flesh leads. Hence, we are plagued with great problems because the flesh is not capable of doing good when it dominates the soul. When, out of love, we deny our own flesh, instead of choosing its cravings, and, in turn, choose God, we move God's mercy to grant our soul grace. We also, in turn, through fasting, can obtain a grace for others, be protected by God from satan, or be granted grace to be cured of all that affects us, such as many things that are among the 60 facts already listed.

The **most important factor** about fasting is that it be done with love. Vicka was asked in August 1995 about headaches associated with fasting. She answered: *When fasting with real love, it is not a problem. Indeed the Pharisees fasted, and if we do the same without love, to what does it avail us?*

The Community at Caritas does an annual fast on bread and water for nine days where the public joins us. (We normally do two or three nine-day bread and water fasts every year.) We started this in 1991, in response to Our Lady's message of August 25, 1991, in which She said:

> **"…I call all of you, dear children, to pray and fast still more firmly. I invite you to renunciation for nine days so that with your help everything I wanted to realize through the secrets I began in Fatima may be fulfilled…"**

After our first nine-day fast, we felt the strength of the novena and its power. Knowing the power of satan and how he constantly works on our weaknesses to bring us down, we decided to annually pray this novena fast to break all the bonds satan has placed on us during the past year, as well as to obtain special graces and specific intentions. Several years ago we did one in which, at the end of the nine days, we spontaneously opened to one of Our Lady's messages, seeking Her words as we ended our fast. We do this in every circumstance we are in, in order to hear Our Lady's words. The message said:

December 18, 1989

> **"The prayers and sacrifices that you decided to offer in these days when I asked you were not done with love. I ask you to offer them with love as during the first days of the apparitions. What you have decided to do and to offer for my intentions during the novena was not enough. You have to choose to give more because you are able."**

Needless to say, upon hearing this we were all disappointed in ourselves. We realized we did not carry it out with the degree of love as we had in the past years. A sign that carried more importance was that our intentions were **not granted**. We, therefore, planned another nine-day fast a month later in order to give ourselves time to recover. This fast was offered with a strong emphasis on love and obedience, first, and then sacrifice. As it was done out of love, rather than "duty" as the first one was, it was very strong. The real joy, upon completion, was our specific intentions were answered, and in a way that exceeded anything we had hoped for. Along with this, a great weight which satan had placed upon us was lifted and broken. It was a very big and humbling lesson for us all, and one in which we learned, without love we would achieve nothing. Our Lady said on December 13, 1984:

> **"...without love you will achieve nothing..."**

Fasting will weaken the body. It will become more tired earlier. It will wish to go to sleep earlier. But at the same time, you will notice the stronger the fast, you are able to maintain — the soul gains strength. You are able to attain deeper prayer, concentrate and meditate stronger. You will have a far greater desire and yearning for God and to do His Will. We, here at Caritas, have noticed that after our Wednesday and Friday fasts of bread and water, the next day we fall more easily into prayer, rather than having to rise up into prayer. Falling requires little effort, rising requires the struggle of climbing. Fasting, supplemented with prayer, changes the next day for us. Our Lady tells us when we go to bed praying, (a fast day is praying all day) we will not be cloudy in our thoughts when we wake up, but will have a clear ability to know Jesus better.

October 30, 1983

> **"If in the evening you fall asleep in peace and in prayer, in the morning you will wake up thinking of Jesus. You will then be able to pray for peace; but if you fall asleep in distraction, the day after will be misty, and you will forget even to pray that day."**

Fasting is the cause of so much good, that as Christians, not to use it would be like having weapons without ammunition. Prayer is the cannon; fasting is the cannon ball; love is the powder, once fired, which sends it. It may seem odd or hard to accept, speaking of prayer, fasting, and love in this way, but all of the following are the exact terminology Our Lady has used in Her messages, especially in regard to satan:

> **"conquer, protect, defend, advance, retreat, attack, guard, armor, battle, defeat, struggle, surrender, drive off, time of battle with satan."** *

These, along with many other words, are clear messages that we are in battle, and **fasting is your ammunition.**

St. John Vianney was hated most by the devil because of his fasting from food and sleep. We are in a great battle, and the weapons we have, such as the Rosary, become much more powerful coupled with fasting.

---

* The following are some message dates in the 21st Edition of Words From Heaven® containing these words in the order read: November 16, 1981; June 25, 1992; September 13, 1984; Before December 26, 1982; July 11, 1985; March 25, 1990; December 25, 1991; October 25, 1984; February 19, 1990; August 8, 1985; July 18, 1985; February 25, 1992; December 25, 1992; July 1983; January 14, 1985; March 18, 1991; March 21, 1988; August 2, 1981; May 23, 1985; September 4, 1986; October 16, 1986.

August 8, 1985

> **"Dear children, today I call you especially now to advance against satan by means of prayer. satan wants to work still more now that you know he is at work. Dear children, put on the armor for battle and with the Rosary in your hand, defeat him! Thank you for having responded to my call."**

You, as an individual, have the power to alter and impact the world. It is a mistake to underestimate the good you bring into the world through your fasting and prayer. **It is time, in this special time, to bring fasting back into the Church; for priests to encourage it; for bishops to preach of it; for them to give examples and witness themselves by doing it. It is to spread over the whole Church and with it will spread the mantle of Our Lady to protect them in leading us, through the Church, into the new time**

Our Lady announced on her Fourteenth Anniversary.

June 25, 1995

> "Dear children! Today I am happy to see you in such great numbers, that you have responded and have come to live my messages. I invite you, little children, to be my joyful carriers of peace in this troubled world. Pray for peace so that as soon as possible <u>a time of peace</u>,* which my heart waits impatiently for, may reign…"

Start the next Wednesday or Friday and watch your life and those around you begin to change. God bless you. Please pray for us. We are doing everything to advance Our Lady's messages, especially in this time, and we depend upon your prayers and

---

* Since this book was originally written, Our Lady has told us that we have entered a new time. Write for a copy of the short book "Entering A New Time" (BK1017) to Caritas of Birmingham, 100 Our Lady Queen of Peace Drive, Sterrett, Alabama 35147, USA. Or download a free copy by going to **mej.com** and click on downloads.

<u>fasting</u> to assist us. We are always thinking of you and praying for you. Always remember, Our Lady has said that the best fast is **bread and water**. Among Our Lady's words in The Field* here in Alabama to us through Marija are the words, **"Go in peace."** Our words are the same to you with the love of Our Lady.

With Love and Affection,

Friend of Medjugorje

---

* The Field is a large meadow between two foothills at the end of the Appalachian Mountains in Alabama. A lone pine tree, a stone altar, and a statue of Our Lady mark the spot where the Queen of Heaven has visited on several occasions through the apparitions of the Medjugorje visionary, Marija Lunetti. It is a Field of conversion, of grace. The Field and the Pine Tree were consecrated to Our Lady before the apparitions first came here in 1988.

However, the primary place of apparitions when Our Lady appeared was in a Friend of Medjugorje's and his wife's bedroom. When Marija came to Alabama, Our Lady said each day where the apparition would be, what time it would take place, and to the surprise of everyone, began giving daily messages.

Our Lady has appeared in the Bedroom of Apparitions 149 times, as of October 28, 2019, through Medjugorje visionary, Marija. It is in this room that Our Lady has shown Her preference to appear in, when Marija visits Caritas. It is the family that is most in need of healing, of which the Bedroom represents.

PART III

A Friend of Medjugorje Answers the Most Asked Questions About Fasting

Throughout the years, a Friend of Medjugorje has been asked many **'how to'** questions regarding fasting. Not only does a Friend of Medjugorje and the Community of Caritas live the fast every week, responding to Our Lady's call to fast every Wednesday and Friday, but several times during the year, they do nine-day fasts on bread and water for special intentions. Below are common questions people often ask A Friend of Medjugorje regarding the nine-day fast. The spirit of these questions and answers apply <u>also</u> to normal fasting on Wednesdays and Fridays. We now share them with you, in hopes that they will give you answers and help you grow stronger in your desire to live the message of fasting. These questions were posed to a Friend of Medjugorje before one of the Community's annual nine-day fasts, in which many across the nation and many from other nations joined us. As mentioned, the Community of Caritas does several nine-day novena fasts yearly, as do individual community members, who sometimes do nine-day fasts on their own when they feel they need it spiritually.

Questions and Answers About Fasting

Fasting is one of the four main messages of Medjugorje. Our Lady said on June 6, 1988:

> **"I ask you to renew in yourselves the messages I have given to you. These are messages of prayer, peace, fasting, and penance. Make some penance yourselves. All of the other messages come from these four basic ones, but also live the other ones."**

* * * * * * * * * * *

The following are real questions asked that a Friend of Medjugorje answers:

Q. Is the fast for 9 consecutive days with no breaks in between?

Friend of Medjugorje: (FOM)
Yes, the nine-day bread and water fast is 9 consecutive days with no breaks in between. (Not even Sunday for the Italians. :)

Q. What are the hours of fasting? Is the fast just from sunrise to sundown, or a full 24-hour day?

FOM: The fast is the full 24-hour day. For example, the Wednesday fast day begins when you wake up in the morning and ends when you go to bed at night—eating only bread and water.

Q. I have a family reunion or other major event during the nine-day fast. Can I break the fast that one day?

FOM: No. The purpose is to sacrifice for a grace. If you could eat normal for an event during the nine-day fast, how much greater would be the grace you receive by attending the event and eating only bread? Our Lady has told us that even though an intention is granted, the more prayer you attach to it, the greater will be the grace connected to the intention granted. Will people notice you are only eating bread? Yes, they may. But, this gives an opportunity to tell them why you are fasting for 9 days. You are not to show off, however, like the Pharisees did. Margaret of Scotland had to attend many formal functions. When she fasted, she would get meager portions and then move the food around her plate as though she was eating, so as to not be noticed. It is understandable at one of your children's weddings you would want to celebrate the joy, but greater would be the grace to fast. Yes, you could also move the dates of the fast (this refers to the annual Caritas fast and the dates designated for it). The option is yours. However, fasting for your intentions with the body of faithful believers across the world, at the same time, before God, has strength. One has free will to do anything. But, the purpose of fasting is to win the greatest amount of grace that God would grant for the fast.

Q. Can I fast on something other than bread and water?

FOM: *Again, one can fast on anything. But Our Lady said on July 21, 1982:*

"The best fast is on bread and water."

The annual nine-day fast in the fall with the Caritas Community is with bread and water.

Q. How much bread can I eat?

FOM: *Our Lady has never given a quantity of bread, She simply said bread and water. For modern man, it is enough that one simply eats only bread. Our Lady did not tell us to starve ourselves. Sometimes people do this when they* *begin to fast. You should eat enough bread to be satisfied. You can be sparse for greater graces, but some who starve themselves lose heart and quit fasting altogether. Both instances are individual choices. The Caritas Community members often skip meals on regular days. It is a part of our life that sometimes circumstances demand that we have to miss a meal. So missing out on bread is not necessarily an issue. But, we find it is better for the fast to make sure we eat bread at breakfast, lunch and dinner. The intention is not to starve yourself, but to offer a sacrifice with a willing heart. Our Lady of Medjugorje gave a message specifically for the Caritas Community on August 26, 1996:*

"Whatever you are doing with the heart, it is all precious to Me."

Be at peace if you need to eat a lot of bread. You will only need to do that for a few days. After the first few days, your body will adjust,

just like God designed it to do, and the fast will become easier.

Q. Can I put butter on my bread?

FOM: *Some may be quick to say that there is nothing wrong with butter on your bread. While this is true, some may need to be more severe when they fast. It is a choice that each individual needs to make, based upon their well-formed conscience and what God is calling them to do. The greater the need for the intention and the greater you strive against yourself and your wants, greater is the grace. Condiments, such as pepper, salt, etc., make bread more flavorful and palatable, but again, if you need a great grace, denying condiments on your bread will make the fast more profound in grace and also strengthen you against vices, weaknesses, etc.*

Q. Can I drink coffee or tea during the fast?

FOM: Again, the purpose of fasting is to make a sacrifice. If you had coffee or tea during the fast, would you be offering an increasing or lessening sacrifice? More importantly, would you be breaking from the things that you cannot do without? Our Lady said on February 25, 1990:

> "…In this season I especially want you to renounce all the things to which you are attached but are hurting your spiritual life. Therefore, little children, decide completely for God, and do not allow satan to come into your life through those things that hurt both you and your spiritual life…"

Our Lady also said on May 25, 1993:

> "I will ask these people to do penance for certain intentions… They will give

up what they cherish the most: drink, coffee, pleasures, television..."

The nine-day fast is to help break from that of which you are attached.

Q. I get bad headaches when I fast. Should I still fast?

FOM: If a woman gets sick when she gets pregnant, does this mean God does not want her to become pregnant? Headaches during a fast are a symptom of your body adjusting to being purified. The body reacts to the sudden loss of caffeine, sugar, etc., and this is not necessarily a bad thing. Drinking plenty of water (lots and lots), even to the point of having to go to the bathroom often, will be a major help when you fast. While spiritually your soul is being purified and your flesh is being "tamed," physically, something else is happening. Your body is releasing toxins when you fast, and water is necessary to flush them out. After about three or four days, usually the severe headaches, stomach aches, etc., tend to go away, even if not entirely, they are often diminished.

Q. What about people with gluten intolerances or with diabetes? Can they fast?

***FOM:** This is something that is happening a lot in recent years. It does not take much to know that we are often poisoned with the food we are eating today. Many doctors and scientists are beginning to speak out that we have the poorest diets that mankind has ever had, though we eat a lot. Many doctors understand that the common causes of the ailments prevalent today are caused by the kinds of food we eat.*

While we will not tell you to fast on bread and water if you are diabetic or have a gluten intolerance, since fasting is a personal choice, what we will tell you, is that some people have joined us for the nine-day fast who are, for example, diabetic, only to see their symptoms go away completely during the fast, and have even been told the sickness itself did not return. We are not doctors. We can only tell you what people have testified to us. Perhaps a step in faith may be what God asks for your healing. Again, this is a personal choice that you, with a well-formed conscience, will need to make on your own. Our Lady said on July 21, 1982:

> **"The best fast is on bread and water… everyone, except the sick, must fast."**

Put into its proper context, we can only guide you in Our Lady's messages. Our Lady, as a Mother, knows not only what is good spiritually for us, but also physically. It makes sense that fasting would also physically be good for us. In this way, Our Lady tells us on August 18, 1982:

> **"…I cannot help him who does not pray and does not sacrifice. The sick,**

just like those who are in good health, must pray and fast for the sick…"

So, Our Lady answers both those who truly cannot fast, and those who, though sick, can still fast.

Q. I tried to fast but it only made me irritable. I don't think Jesus and Our Lady would want me to fast and be irritable. Don't you think so?

__FOM:__ How is one person in a wheelchair of a joyful disposition, and another of a bitter disposition? One's heart is the problem. Because something may be difficult does not excuse you for being uncharitable. You sin against charity when doing so. Fasting is to conquer your faults. If you get irritable by fasting, you are also getting irritable at other things when you do not fast. Fasting is not only for an intention; it is to give joy to your life and to acquire virtues. Our Lady said on August 15, 1983:

"Every disorder comes from satan... satan is enraged against those who fast and those who are converted."

So, when you decide to fast, satan is enraged against you. You collaborate with his rage by allowing yourself to get irritable. Jesus said that when you fast, you should not change your appearance and look gloomy, but rather comb your hair, and look like you are not fasting. Therefore, you are not excused to be irritable. The purpose of fasting is to tame your passions. Irritability is not a disposition from God, it is from satan. Are you lying to yourself in looking for a way to get out of having to fast? If you must, go to Confession every day of the fast. Instead of making an excuse, make yourself better during the fast and you will not be irritable when you are not fasting. Your heart will learn the virtues of being peaceful all the time.

Q. I heard that Catholics do not fast on Sunday. The nine-day fast would require us to fast on Sunday. What should I do?

FOM: Fast on Sunday. We live in an age where the norm is not the norm. What might have been okay 50 years or 100 years ago is not okay today. Our Lady said on March 18, 2003:

> **"…Particularly at this holy time of penance and prayer, I call you to make a choice…"**

The choice before us is whether we are hearing and listening to the call to change our lives. While the norm, in the past, was that many Catholics did not fast on Sunday in honor of the Resurrection, in this particular time, in this age, Our Lady needs our prayers and sacrifices. Our Lady of Medjugorje said in May 1984:

> "...Fasting has been forgotten during the last quarter of the century within the Catholic Church."

Q. I really love bread and it would not be much of a sacrifice. I wonder if I should fast on something else?

FOM: Nice try. But, everyone gets tired of the same kind of food. The Israelites loved the taste of the manna from Heaven, but they eventually began to grumble, "Is this all we have to eat?" If you really love bread, you will get to the point where you get a little tired of it during the nine-day fast.

Q. I know that I will be really tired during the nine-day fast. Should I limit my activities during the nine-day fast?

FOM: Often nine-day fasts are during some of our busiest times at Caritas. We can tell you from experience that the last thing you want is to be idle, or have a lot of free time. You do not want to find yourself staring at the refrigerator. You should keep yourself busy, keep yourself active, cleaning, volunteering, for example, at a soup kitchen, etc. In reality, you will find that if you are drinking enough water, after about three or four days, your energy level will rise, even though towards the night, you may feel sleepy. Not only will you spiritually feel light, but also it has been our experience that physically you will feel better because you are not being weighed down by lots of food.

Q. I am pregnant. Should I fast? What does the Community do?

FOM: *Pregnancy is not a sickness. The world looks upon this in the wrong way, but God has programmed this as a beautiful gift. In ages past, it was common that bread was the only thing to eat. Many pregnant women found themselves in this kind of situation. However, this having been said, there are* *responsibilities with carrying a life within you. This would include proper nutrition. The mothers of the Community, when pregnant, make sacrifices by eating minimal healthy foods that they do not like, like liver, no sweets, eating more measured, making more nutritious bread, etc. It is a way of sharing in the sacrifice while, at the same time, keeping their responsibilities towards the life God has given them to carry. God designed the body to tell you exactly what it needs. Some pregnant women may be able to go without eating between meals, while others may not be able to do that. You can join in the sacrifice while still keeping your responsibility towards the life within you.*

Q. What about our children? How old should they be to fast?

FOM: *Medjugorje visionary, Jakov Colo, was included by Our Lady at 10 years of age* *to fast with the other five visionaries. In our Community, we have had children down to six or seven years old fast for nine days. Because all the Community fasts, the children go day by day eating what we eat, running around playing , etc., as if it is nothing. They do not complain because they are raised and witnessed to by the older youth and adults. In all fasts, all children, even down to young children give up sweets, sugar cereals, and drink only water (except babies), etc. Therefore, they are raised in a spirit of offering to God in sacrificing. It is very normal and helps them to understand and appreciate the gift of food and to have more sensitivity of what it would be like without the food we are blessed with.*

Q. I want to fast but it would make my husband mad. What should I do?

FOM: *The Scripture says that obedience is greater than sacrifice. If your husband forbids* *it, then you will do more by your obedience to him than by fasting. But, there again, you can be very measured in what you eat. You could skip what you crave most and eat at each meal what you care for the least. If however, your husband does not forbid it outright, then you can do your fasting in secret. One woman wrote to us and said that she went the entire nine days fasting on bread and water. She knew her husband would not necessarily like it, so she did it in secret. She cooked normal meals, sat down with her husband, put food on her plate and acted like she was eating, like Margaret of Scotland, already mentioned. Her husband never said a word about it. On the morning after the nine-day fast ended, she sat down to have a cup of coffee with her husband, took her first sip and said, "Ah, this coffee is so good!" Her husband turned to her and asked, "Are you done with that fast yet?" She was shocked and told us, "My husband's so smart!"*

But, because of her disposition, she did not anger him. Our Lady calls us to the same. Our Lady said in July 1985:

> **"...Carry my messages with humility, in such a way that on seeing happiness in you, persons will desire to be like you. Do not carry my messages to simply throw them to others."**

We will tell you that if you throw fasting at your husband, if you beat your husband over the head with fasting, you will lose. He will not be interested in you, your fast, or what you believe. Instead, following Our Lady's words, you will gain his admiration.

Q. How much does it cost to sign up for the nine-day fast? (Caritas of Birmingham leads a nine-day fast annually in the fall of each year).

FOM: To sign up for the nine-day fast, it only costs the sacrifice of eating bread and drink-

ing water. There is no monetary cost to join the fast, though we recommend that the money saved for meals during the fast, is given to God as a tithe. We always fund these types of initiatives ourselves.

Q. I struggle with fasting, so should I even try to do a nine-day fast on bread and water?

FOM: *When you join the Caritas Community in a nine-day fast, you join thousands of others who have also committed to the fast in the past and present and, therefore, you gain grace from our collective efforts. We have many testimonies from people like you who were hesitant to sign up for the nine-day fast, but after making the decision to try, felt they were carried by grace throughout the fast. Their willingness to try, even though their faith was small, won for them the grace to succeed. Start with making a firm decision in prayer, and then see the many ways Our Lady will come to your aid to en-*

courage you and increase your faith until you reach the finish line. When you finally break your fast after day nine, no amount of cheating compares to how good the food tastes after giving Our Lady this sacrifice. But the joy of knowing your spirit conquered your flesh and then to receive the answer to your prayers is even sweeter.

Incredible Spiritual Benefits!

Incredible Physical Benefits!

A Friend of Medjugorje updated this short book with some amazing findings that he always believed would be discovered in the DNA of fasting but up until now was not revealed. He has always maintained that Our Lady would not be asking us to fast for spiritual benefits without there also being good fruit for our physical benefit and well-being. Discovering the following research will excite you as much as it did him.

PART IV

New Supplement (as of September 2016)

How to Radically Increase Your Intermittent Fasting Success

The following is by Dr. Joseph Mercola. Though his study 'is secular,' he states purely why all need to fast for physical health. His findings are astounding, all the way down to Dr. Mercola recognizing the best fast is **two days a week!** His assertions are only from a scientific viewpoint, yet they are amazing in that they completely show Our Lady's advise for the soul's benefit, benefits the body as well. In 1986, at the beginning of Caritas, a priest stated that fasting on bread and water all day is dangerous. It was responded back to him that, *"It is impossible for Our Lady to tell us to fast, and it be harmful. In fact, because Our Lady so strongly speaks about fasting twice a week, there also has to be some kind of physical consequences of good for our bodies, as well as for our souls."* After you read Dr. Mercola's dissertation on fasting, you will not only agree, but will be amazed at what you will learn. Dr. Mercola states:

> *"Do you want to live to be at least 100 like I do? This is quite achievable today, but living that long loses much of its appeal if you aren't healthy for the duration.*
>
> **"One excellent tool for increasing both health AND longevity is intermittent fasting, i.e. an eating schedule in which you feast on some days and dramatically cut your consumption on others.**
>
> *"One of the downsides to the modern Western lifestyle is eating too frequently, which makes*

your body lazy about performing its repair and rejuvenation operations. Intermittent fasting effectively mimics the eating habits of our ancestors, who did not have access to grocery stores or food around the clock.

"They cycled through periods of feast and famine, and modern research shows this cycling imparts a number of health benefits, such as improved cardiovascular health, better metabolic function, and reduced cancer risk.

You do not want weak or damaged immune cells to reproduce. You want them to die out so they will not continue weak generations. This parallels nature. The weak deer in a deer herd die out, leaving only the strongest to reproduce, thereby strengthening the deer herd. It is a practice in a cow herd. The farmer will cull out every year the bottom performing 5% of the herd to strengthen the traits of cows who are not sickly, who gain weight easier, are gentle, who breed more successfully, resist disease, among many other improvements. This is why the weaker cells are culled out by fasting. It improves your health when only the most healthy cells are dividing and becoming more populated to work in your body! Our Lady knows what you need spiritually and physically!!

—Friend of Medjugorje

"A study published in the publication Cell Stem Cell[1] discovered that intermittent fasting causes your body to beef up your immune system by getting rid of damaged white blood cells and replacing them with new ones, shifting stem cells from a dormant state to a state of self-renewal. Fasting essentially hits your body's "reset button."

"Researchers from the University of Southern California found that during prolonged fasting, your white blood count drops, but when you resume eating, this count goes up.

"Upon investigating this phenomenon, researchers found that people's bodies were purging out the old, damaged immune cells, and then replacing them with new healthy ones.

"The fasting cycle appears to flip on a "regenerative switch," triggering a key gene controlling the enzyme PKA. During fasting, PKA

is reduced, which flips on this regenerative switch that sends your body's stem cells into action.

"The scientists believe their findings have major implications for healthier aging and are investigating the possibility that these benefits are applicable to many different systems and organs, beyond your immune system. The study's co-author, Valter Longo, said:

> 'We could not predict that prolonged fasting would have such a remarkable effect in promoting stem cell-based regeneration of the hematopoietic system.'"[2]

Fasting is Good for Your Heart, Brain and Waistline

"Fasting is commonplace throughout history and has been used as part of various spiritual practices for millennia. But modern science now tells us that fasting actually offers a number of health benefits, including the following:

"Normalizing your insulin and leptin sensitivity, and boosting mitochondrial energy efficiency: *One of the primary mechanisms making intermittent fasting so beneficial for your health is related to its impact on insulin and leptin sensitivity. While sugar is a source of energy for your body, it also causes insulin/leptin resistance when consumed excessively.*

"Insulin/leptin resistance, in turn, is a primary driver of chronic disease – from heart disease to type 2 diabetes to cancer. Intermittent fasting helps retrain your body to use fat as its primary fuel.

"Mounting evidence confirms that when your body becomes adapted to burning fat instead of sugar, your disease risk dramatically drops. Fasting also normalized ghrelin levels, known as "the hunger hormone." Another boon of intermittent fasting is that it helps eliminate sugar cravings.

"Promoting Human Growth Hormone production (H. G. H.): *Research has shown that fasting can raise* **H**u*man* **G**r*owth* **H**o*rmone by as much as 1,300 percent in women, and 2,000 percent in men.*[3] *Human Growth Hormone plays an important part in health, fitness, and slowing the aging process. It's also a fat-burning hormone, which helps explain why fasting is so conducive to weight loss.*

"Lowering triglyceride levels and improving other biomarkers of disease.

> Our Lady tells us to alternate fast days—fast Wednesday, skip Thursday and fast on Friday
>
> —Friend of Medjugorje

"**Reducing oxidative stress:** *Fasting decreases the accumulation of oxidative radicals in the cell, thereby reducing oxidative damage to cellular proteins, lipids, and nucleic acids associated with aging and disease.*

"**Protects your brain:** *Fasting boosts the production of a protein called* **B**rain-**D**erived **N**eurotrophic **F**actor (B. D. N. F.), *stimulating the release of new brain cells and triggering numerous other chemicals that protect you from the changes associated with Alzheimer's and Parkinson's disease.*

"Research suggests **alternate-day** *fasting, restricting your meals on fasting days to about 600 calories, can boost the* **B**rain-**D**erived **N**eurotrophic **F**actor by 50 to 400 percent, depending on the region of the brain.*[4]

"Animal research shows that fasting has a beneficial impact on longevity by several mechanisms, including improved insulin sen-

sitivity and inhibition of the mTOR pathway. Intermittent fasting is also one of the most effective ways to shed unwanted fat. When your body doesn't need sugar as its primary fuel, you'll experience fewer cravings when your sugar stores run low.

"Some warn that intermittent fasting may result in loss of lean body mass, but I have not found this to be true. Dr. Krista Varaday, assistant professor of Kinesiology and Nutrition at the University of Illinois, has conducted numerous studies on intermittent fasting and has found that 90 percent of the weight people lose is body fat, with only 10 percent being lean body mass.[5] <u>Moving throughout the day</u> and consuming an appropriate amount of high-quality protein will help minimize loss of muscle mass.

The 5:2 Intermittent Fasting Plan

"Intermittent fasting is an umbrella term that covers a wide array of fasting schedules. As a general rule, it involves cutting calories in whole or in part, either a couple of days per week, every other day, or even daily. Dr. Michael Mosley became so convinced of the health benefits of intermittent fasting that he wrote a book on the subject, <u>The Fast Diet: Lose Weight, Stay Healthy, and Live Longer with the Simple Secret of Intermittent Fasting</u>.[6]

"The fasting schedule he suggests is to eat normally for five days per week, then fast for two, which is referred to as the 5:2 intermittent fasting plan. On fasting days, he recommends cutting your food <u>down to one-fourth of your normal daily caloric intake</u>, or about 600 calo-

ries for men and about 500 for women, along with plenty of water and tea. Dr. Mosley reports having lost 19 pounds in two months by following this 5:2 intermittent fasting plan.

It really doesn't matter which days you choose as your fasting days. Monday is a good place to start if you're fired up at the beginning of a new week or if you've had a "calorific" weekend. On a fasting day, you can spread your 500/600 calories throughout the day, or you might choose to enjoy them all at an evening meal. Just find the routine that works best for you. Dr. Mosley offers three "golden rules" for success:[7]

1. *Be sensible on non-fasting days. Eat normally, enjoy treats in moderation, but avoid bingeing.*

2. *Watch what you drink. Juices, lattes, alcohol, fizzy drinks, and smoothies typically*

contain a glut of calories and sugar, but won't satisfy your appetite.

3. *Try adding another fasting day. Go for a 4:3 pattern (four days of normal eating, three days of reduced calories). Or even use alternate-day fasting, which can really bump up your weight loss over the course of a few months, especially if you exercise.*

My Personal Recommendations
(Dr. Mercola)
[And Insulin Problems]

"The version of intermittent fasting that I recommend for nearly anyone with insulin resistance is simply to restrict your eating to a specific window of time every day, such as an eight-hour window. I have experimented with different schedules for the past three years, and this is my personal preference, as it's really easy to comply with once your body has made the shift from burning sugar to burning fat for its primary fuel. Fat, being a slow-burning fuel, allows you to keep going without suffering from the dramatic energy crashes associated with sugar. And if you're not hun-

gry, then not eating for several hours is no big deal!

"You do this every day until your insulin/ leptin resistance improves and your health issues resolve, such as suboptimal weight, blood pressure, blood sugar, etc. After that, just do it as often as you need to maintain your healthy state. I initially used a six-hour eating window, but now I use a 10- to 11-hour window, and I rarely eat anything during the four hours prior to going to bed. I disagree with claims that you can eat whatever you want on non-fasting days. If your goal is optimal health (not just weight loss), you simply cannot achieve this without a high-quality diet. In terms of what to eat on non-fasting days, I recommend following these five basic guidelines:

- *Avoid junk food, processed food, and sugar-laden drinks.*

- *Limit your **fruit** consumption until your weight and health have normalized, especially fruits high in fructose.*

- *Replace starchy, carbohydrate-rich foods with healthy fats such as coconut oil, olive oil, olives, butter, eggs, avocados, and nuts (macadamia nuts are particularly beneficial, as they are high in fat and low in protein)*

- *Consume protein moderately, making sure your animal products (meat, eggs, dairy) come from organic, pasture-raised animals.*

- *Include naturally fermented foods (fermented vegetables, yogurt, kefir, miso, etc.) in your diet, which are extremely beneficial for your digestive tract, immune system, and just about every other aspect of your health.*

Who Should use Extra Caution When Fasting, or Avoid It Altogether?

"Intermittent fasting is appropriate for most people, but there are certain individuals who should exercise some extra caution. If you fall into any of the following five categories, my recommendation would be to focus on improving your overall nutrition instead of implementing a fasting schedule.

- *Hypoglycemia*
- *Diabetes*
- *Severe chronic stress (adrenal fatigue)*
- *Cortisol dysregulation*
- *Pregnant or nursing mothers*

"Hypoglycemia is a condition characterized by tendencies toward abnormally low blood sugar. It's commonly associated with

diabetes, but you can be hypoglycemic even if you're not diabetic. Common symptoms of a hypoglycemic crash include headache, weakness, tremors, irritability, and hunger. As your blood glucose levels continue to plummet, more severe symptoms can set in, such as confusion or abnormal behavior, visual disturbances, seizures, and loss of consciousness.

"One of the keys to preventing hypoglycemia is eliminating excess sugars (especially processed fructose) and grains from your diet, and replacing them with high-quality proteins and fats. Keep in mind that it will take some time for your blood sugar to normalize. If you're prone to hypoglycemia, instead for fasting, just work on optimizing your overall diet until your blood sugar levels are stable. Once you've achieved this, then you can gradually begin experimenting with fasting.

"Pregnant or nursing mothers should avoid fasting, as there is no research thus far to support its benefit. Your baby needs plenty of nutrients, during and after birth. If you're pregnant, make sure to include naturally fermented foods to optimize your and your baby's gut flora.

"If you have chronically elevated stress, then chances are your cortisol is dysregulated. Chronic stress can inflict severe long-term damage to your health, so it's imperative that you find a way to manage it."

End Dr. Mercola

End Notes:
1. Cell Stem Cell June 5, 2014
2. Medical Daily, January 5, 2015
3. EurekAlert! April 3, 2011
4. Washington Post, December 31, 2012
5. CBS News, April 4, 2014
6. BBC News, January 2, 2013
7. Daily Mail, January 5, 2015

* * * * * * *

The following letter was sent to a Friend of Medjugorje in response to his answers to fasting, included in this short book. It is added as encouragement for those who desire to fast, but are stopped because of health concerns or issues.

Dear Friend of Medjugorje,

"I read your responses to questions on Mej. com regarding Fasting and agree whole heartedly with the wisdom in the answers. I am one who is struggling with a chronic illness that, at present, limits by ability to fast strictly on bread and water. That said, I write to encourage others who may have health problems or problems with gluten, to follow in faith what you have written. Medical doctor's recommendations are generally good to follow, though they are likely considering only the person's physical health with a secular view, rather than a Biblical view. I believe we have

the "Doctor of doctors" coming to earth daily Who has given medicine and instructions to heal body <u>and</u> soul. From experience, I would encourage anyone struggling with illness to pray for Our Lady to help you fast, and to "Let your body stop you, don't you stop your body." In other words, on Wednesdays and Fridays begin the day consecrating your fast to Our Lady and making a decision to fast on bread and water. If throughout the day you find that bread alone is not possible, then you can prayerfully evaluate your steps from there. As you, a Friend of Medjugorje have said, the most important part of fasting is prayer.

"Our Lady said March 25, 2007,

> **'…I desire to inspire you to continue to live fasting with an open heart. By fasting and renunciation, little children, you will be stronger in faith…'**

*"Thank you, Friend of Medjugorje and the Community of Caritas for your courageous witness in fasting and sacrifice. I have made progress in the spiritual life, **become stronger in faith**, and overcome difficult trials, not through homilies, or the gentle guidelines for fasting during Lent, but by drawing strength from the writings and witness of a Friend of Medjugorje. You are the only one I have heard give common sense answers that curb excuses disguising fear or spiritual laziness. I feel you are the voice for Our Lady, Who truly is looking out for the spiritual welfare of Her children, as well as their physical welfare. My goal is to keep fasting until I am able to fast on bread and water again for a full day, and one day join your Community and those around the world in a nine-day bread and water fast again."*

A note from a Friend of Medjugorje as an addition to the above letter:

Doctors have told people, *"You will never walk again."* Yet, there are those who are determined to overcome this restriction, putting their faith in God, and working towards this goal. God, seeing their faith, has given some the grace to confound medical prognosis and walk again, while giving others interior strength to become witnesses of perseverance to others. You may find the same to be true with fasting as Our Lady's apostle. Medjugorje visionary, Ivan once said, *"Fasting without prayer is like a soldier with only one leg. He is easily defeated."* To walk in the spiritual life as Our Lady's apostle takes prayer <u>and</u> fasting. So keep trying!

Legal Disclaimer

The subject matter contained in this book is given with the understanding that neither the author nor the publisher is engaged to render legal, medical, or other health-related advice. Since your situation is fact-dependent, you may wish to additionally seek the services of an appropriately licensed medical professional.

Important

This is the original recipe for the bread. What follows in the next 35 pages is an apprenticeship of how to bake the bread, explaining in detail the process of making it. Through this teaching lesson, you will learn the right way to make this bread and how much fun and consolation baking bread can be. Once you learn how to make it, this one sheet will be enough to follow.

Colafrancesco's Italian Bread Recipe
Makes approximately 10 loaves

INGREDIENTS (Double everything for the large recipe that yields approximately 20 loaves on the following pages):

- (8) c./1.9 L very warm water
- (2) Packs of yeast/4.5 tsp./14 g dissolved in ¾ c. /177mL of water
- (4) Tbs./68.25 g salt (overflowing)
- (1) Tbs./15 mL honey (overflowing)
- (1½) Tbs./18.75 g granulated sugar
- (2½) Tbs./37.5 mL Wesson oil (good quality vegetable oil)
- (4) eggs (buy a dozen, you will need more for glazing the loaves)
- (¼) tsp./1 g ascorbic acid
- (2) tsp./7 g malt powder (overflowing)
- (1) lb./16 oz/454 g salted butter
- (1) 5 lb bag /2.27 kg "King Arthur Unbleached Bread Flour"*
- (1) 5 lb bag/2.27 kg "Gold Medal Better For Bread Unbleached Flour"*

* For European or foreign countries use "Unbleached, not self-rising, bread flour."

DIRECTIONS *(This is not sufficient unless you have already read the following 35 pages)*: Dissolve yeast in bowl with a little honey or sugar and stir. Add ascorbic acid and malt powder. Add flour to liquid mixture. Do not stir all the flour in at once. Form dough into a ball and cover dough ball with oil. Cover with plastic and set in warm place to rise. Allow two risings, punching down in between. When dough is ready, place into bread pans. Allow to rise. Cover with egg mixture (see pages 117–121). Bake at 450°F/232°C for 10 minutes then turn down the oven to 375°F/190°C and continue to bake for 25 minutes or longer. Use your judgement to adjust the temperature according to how your oven cooks. Cook the bread to taste, not just by the recipe.

Colafrancesco's Italian Bread Recipe

"Give us this day our daily bread."

The Colafrancesco Italian Bread Recipe is well over 100 years old, perhaps centuries old, handed down through the family from one generation to the next. For this reason, it is a heritage that cultivates love; love within the family, love of bread, and love of fasting. A Friend of Medjugorje, through living Our Lady's messages, has enculturized this love into a "way of life," and now shares this generational recipe, that others might be able to create rich traditions within families of their own.

Tony Frank Colafrancesco sitting in the Colafrancesco family bread pan (1924). Generations of one single family have eaten thousands of loaves of bread over three centuries out of the same pan.

The Richness of a Bread Pan

This bread pan has a rich history, passing from one generation to the next. Its legacy has spanned across three centuries: from the 1800's, 1900's and into the 21st century, while passing through the hands of four generations of Colafrancescos, since 1890.

A Friend of Medjugorje's Italian great-grandmother, "Mamalene" (Madilene) was born in 1895. Her parents brought this bread pan with them from southern Italy to Colorado where it served both as bread pan for the family and bath pan for Mamalene. Twenty-nine years later, in 1924, Mamalene's first born son of ten children, Tony Frank Colafrancesco (a Friend of Medjugorje's father, pictured left), continued the family tradition, taking all his baths, for his first six months, in this bread pan. A Friend of Medjugorje states:

"Bread has always been an important part of our family life. Bread, the Bread of Life, really symbolizes the richness of what it makes in the families. All the bread that has come through this bread pan, amounts to thousands of loaves of

bread, and has fed four generations whose babies also bathed in it.

"This bread pan is handed down through the hands of the oldest Colafrancesco grandson, keeping it as a heritage within the lineage. It is a sacred relic of blood, of family, of tradition. It hands down and speaks of a recipe that journeyed from Italy, seeking, and feeding a way of life, transitioning and embracing a new way of life in America.

"Few people today desire to live like this. There is little purpose to the seriousness of life. Everything is a 'throw away' society today. We don't keep anything. There is no reverence to where you come from or where you are going. People have no meaning to their life. This bread pan adds dimension to life, to the family, by its meaning and purpose. They know where they come from, and when walking with Our Lady, they know where they are going."

~ Friend of Medjugorje

Tony Louis Colafrancesco II, pictured above in November 2014, is the great-great-grandson of Mamalene and the great-grandson of Tony Frank Colafrancesco pictured on page 94. Little Tony, six months old, sits in the bread pan, at about the same age his great-grandfather was ninety years earlier. The dual purpose of a bread pan continues its legacy in the Colafrancesco family. **Buy yourself a bread pan and begin a spiritual and physical legacy tradition.**

~ A Note from the Community of Caritas ~

Bread making is a special tradition in the Community of Caritas, cultivated by the witness of a Friend of Medjugorje who, in an Italian home, grew up loving bread. His mother would make bread every Friday, in their family bread pan. Within this recipe, you will see pictures to inspire you in creating your own memories. A Friend of Medjugorje remembers some of his own:

"When bread came out of the oven, mom would load a couple of us up in the car with a warm loaf of bread and drive the mile to the rectory of our parish church, Blessed Sacrament Church. I would get out of the car, carrying the bread and knock on the door. Monsignor Keys would take it from my hands, smell it, kiss it, and smile and wave to my mom behind the steering wheel. When we came home from school our snack was Italian bread, which we loved. When we came home from church on Sunday, it was so good to walk in the house and smell the 'suga' simmering (pasta sauce). We would grab a piece of bread and dip it in the 'suga' sauce to eat. We would do this two or three times each. Dad did it too, and momma encouraged it. Having taken a loaf of the week's batch of bread from the freezer and heated out of the oven, was more than we could resist when the smell filled the kitchen. These positive memories taught us to be happy now about fasting today and the good grace that comes with it."

Colafrancesco's Italian Bread Recipe

Large Batch Recipe
Yields Approximately 20 Large Loaves

For Smaller Batches, Use Same Steps

Before making, read the entire recipe first to familiarize yourself with the important details. Otherwise, you will make mistakes which will affect the bread.

Grocery List

- (2) 5 lb bags/2.27 kg "King Arthur Unbleached Bread Flour"*
- (2) 5 lb bags/2.27 kg "Gold Medal Better For Bread Unbleached Flour"*
- (16) c./3.8 L very warm water
- (2) Tbs./30 mL honey
- (3) Tbs./37.5 g granulated sugar
- (5) Tbs. Wesson oil/75 mL (good quality vegetable oil)
- (16) eggs (buy 2 dozen, you may use more for glazing the loaves)
- (8) Tbs./136.5 g salt
- (4) packs active dry yeast/9 tsp. /28 g
- (½) tsp./2 g ascorbic acid
- (4) tsp./14 g malt powder
- (1) lb./16 oz./454 g salted butter
- (20) large loaf pans to bake the bread in
- (1) large trash bag to cover dough while rising

---

* For European or foreign countries use "Unbleached, not self-rising, bread flour."

Preparation Before Mixing the Ingredients

I. At least 30 minutes before beginning, pre-heat the oven to 150°F/66°C and put in the following ingredients to get them warm, so as to not cool down the yeast temperature when you begin mixing.

   a. flour
   b. oil
   c. eggs

Note: *__Be sure to monitor your ingredients while they are in the oven.__ The eggs are warmed to get the chill out of them, and to maintain the yeast's temperature. Take them out as soon as they are room temperature or slightly warm. The flour will take longer to warm up. If you aren't in a hurry, you can pre-heat your oven to 135°F / 57°C to begin, although beginning at this temperature will take longer for the ingredients to warm. If you are in a hurry, and don't have time to wait, you can set the oven to 150°F / 66°C, but be sure to watch your ingredients so they don't get too hot.*

Part I – The Yeast

In making Colafrancesco's Italian Bread, the yeast is critical to do correctly. Everything else is forgiving, but not the yeast. If you fail to do this right, the bread will not be good. If the yeast does not rise properly, the bread will be packed. A mixture too cool slows yeast growth; too hot kills yeast. You must be at the right general temperature and maintain the warmth of the ingredients throughout the process of making the dough, and also while rising. This is why you pre-warm the ingredients, so that as you add them they will not cool down the yeast. Many people fail at this one point of keeping the temperature generally correct. It is part of the learning curve to making this bread. Keep trying and you will improve the more you make it.

<u>Yeast Ingredients:</u>

1½ c./355 mL warm, but not hot water.
9 tsp./28 g active dry yeast
1 heaping tsp./5–7 mL honey

<u>Yeast Prep:</u>

Warm a glass measuring cup or bowl that the yeast will rise in. Make sure the bowl for mixing the water, yeast and honey is warm before adding these ingredients.

<u>Step 1 – Making the Yeast</u>

Yeast grows best between 105°F / 41°C and begins to die at 115°F / 46°C. Anything cooler or hotter will stunt or kill the yeast. In the beginning of making this bread you may want to use a thermometer. With practice you'll learn by feel.

a. Place 1½ c./355 mL warm water in bowl. We even warm the bowl. Test the water. It should feel very warm but not hot to the touch.

b. Add yeast to the water.

c. Add 1 heaping teaspoon/5 mL honey.

d. Stir all ingredients using a wooden spoon until the honey dissolves.

e. Place on stove top, on open oven door, or warm place.

f. Let the yeast rise. There will be a lot foam on top that should be airy and fluffy.

"Fasting, coupled with prayer, is one of the most powerful things that can happen. Fasting, coupled with prayer, will attain everything you ask for. These are Our Lady's words. You want to walk close to God? You fast."

~Friend of Medjugorje

In the kitchen of their grandfather and grandmother, two of a Friend of Medjugorje's grandchildren, Victoria and Faith, are the newest, among the generations of Colafrancesco's, to learn the art and love of making their family's Italian bread. A Friend of Medjugorje has brought this joyful witness into his family and the Community of Caritas of always letting the children help, just as his parents let he and his brothers and sister do the same. The children will want to eat the dough, etc. It is around the bread pan they will learn to love bread. Often before baking the loaves, we will fry some of the dough in a frying pan with butter which the children always like.

Colafrancesco's Italian Bread Recipe

Part II – The Dough

Note: *It is <u>very important</u> not to use any scented dish soap to wash your hands or rinse dishes with while making this recipe, as the scent from the soap will stay on your hands and affect the flavor of your dough and bread. Also, make sure any dishtowels you use to dry your hands or dishes with do not have any scent to them from fabric softeners etc. Do not cover the dough or baked loaves of bread with a dish towel that has been washed with fabric softener or fragrant detergent, as the dough/bread will absorb the scent very quickly.*

Ingredients:

- (16) c./3.8 L very warm water
- (8) Tbs./136.5 g salt (overflowing)
- (2) Tbs./30 mL honey (overflowing)
- (3) Tbs./37.5 g granulated sugar
- (5) Tbs./75 mL Wesson oil
- (8) eggs
- (½) tsp./2 g ascorbic acid
- (4) tsp./14 g malt powder (overflowing)
- (2) 5 lb bag/80 oz/2.27 kg "King Arthur Unbleached Bread Flour"*
- (2) 5 lb bag/80 oz/2.27 kg "Gold Medal Better For Bread Unbleached Flour"*
- Risen Yeast (see Part I, pg. 78)

---

* For European or foreign countries use "Unbleached, not self-rising, bread flour."

Step 1 Prep:

a. Before you begin mixing the ingredients in the bread pan, heat up the pan to the same general temperature as the other ingredients. We usually let hot water sit in the pan to warm the pan while the yeast rises in another place. See step 6 on page 108. To be repetitious, it is important that this bowl be very warm, so that the ingredients are at a consistent temperature throughout the recipe. When you're ready, dump the water out and start putting the measured warm water and ingredients in the pan.

Step 1 — Water and Salt:

a. In the large metal pan, combine the warm water and salt.

b. Mix with your hands until the salt is dissolved

c. Taste the mixture. It should taste <u>very</u> salty. Later on, the salty taste will be cut down when combined with the flour etc. The right amount of salt is important. Too little salt and the bread will taste flat, too much salt and the bread will taste salty.

Step 2 — Eggs, Oil, Honey and Sugar

a. Beat the eggs well with a fork in a separate bowl.

b. Add the eggs to the salt water mixture and mix with your hands.

c. Add the oil

d. Add the honey

e. Add the sugar

f. Mix all the ingredients together with your hands until all are dissolved.

g. Taste the mixture and adjust ingredients if necessary. This will take experience through time to know what it should taste like.

Step 3 — Yeast

a. Pour the yeast in while the ingredients are mostly liquid in the pan. It is not necessary for there to be any flour in the pan when you pour the yeast.

b. Blend the yeast into the mixture with your hands until well mixed.

c. Taste the mixture (You should be able to lightly taste the yeast.)

"Our Lady wants you to fast out of love for Her, for Her plans, and She will reciprocate by interceding before God to win every grace necessary for you to come in union and to have a heart of love and to feel a real peace. Fasting brings peace."

~ Friend of Medjugorje

Victoria gets ready to pour in the yeast while Faith prepares to stir it in. The picture makes it look like the flour is already heavily mixed in. It is not. A Way of Life brings joys and makes memories that live on generationally. For those who have grown up around the bread pan, fasting can be a special joy once one becomes an adult. It is easy never to complain about fasting, rather to witness your fasting with love. The children of the Community of Caritas grow up with a positive mentality of the adults who witness this positive attitude. A Friend of Medjugorje formed the Community adults to have this attitude, which, when passed on to children is a gift that they will have their whole lifetime. Learning how to make the bread they love, with people they love, is added sweetness for them. How sad for those who reject Our Lady's call to bread and water fasting to not have these joys. It will be more difficult for them later in life to incorporate fasting into a way of life.

Step 4 — Ascorbic Acid

a. Add the ascorbic acid to the mixture and mix in with your hands

Step 5 — Malt

a. Add the malt powder. The malt will form clumps. Break the clumps of malt up into the mixture with your hands and blend in slightly.

b. Make sure no malt sticks to the bottom of the bowl.

Step 6 — Adding Flour to the Liquid Mixture

a. Pour the liquid mixture into the warm mixing bowl

b. Add (1) 5 lb bag/2.27 kg of flour at a time, beginning and ending with the King Arthur Flour.* Example: Bag #1 — King Arthur, bag #2 & 3 — Gold Medal, Bag #4 — King Arthur

---

* For European or foreign countries use "Unbleached, not self-rising, bread flour."

"You will not be hurt. You are not giving up anything. You are gaining something. You will always gain from fasting."

~ Friend of Medjugorje

The finesse of a mother is taught to her children through imitation and practice. A Friend of Medjugorje's wife, Annette, teaches her grandchildren more than making bread. Don't think you won't make a mess, you will! It will be on the table, on the floor, everywhere. It's part of making bread.

"Our Lady desires fasting to be a routine part of your way of life, for life. Pray for the gift of fasting."

~ Friend of Medjugorje

c. Mix by hand until dough becomes tacky and begins to stick to your fingers. Often there will be many hands in the bread pan, as you see a Friend of Medjugorje's hand, his wife's hand and two of his grandchildren.

Note: You may not use all of the bags of flour before the dough is at the correct consistency. It always varies.

    d. When the dough is done, it should form a ball. It should not be sticky. Keep kneading the dough by hand, until it is mixed and a little tacky.

    e. Taste some of the dough, to learn the flavor of what it should taste like.

At this point, you may be thinking, "I'll never use 20 loaves of bread! Why such a large recipe?" You can cut the recipe down, but we usually make big batches. A Friend of Medjugorje's parents made this recipe every Friday, and the family would go through all the loaves in a week! However, if you don't use all 20 loaves, they freeze very well and taste like fresh homemade bread when heated up and brought back to life. There's nothing better than taking a loaf of Italian bread, pulling the inside white out and dipping it in the yellow center of a fried egg. It's delicious. Whether eaten alone with dinner or used for Italian sausage sandwiches etc., or Sunday pasta, you always have homemade bread to offer family and friends…or to take with you on your travels as a Friend of Mejugorje's father did.

> *"The first time my dad went to Medjugorje, my brother and I noticed that he was carrying on board the plane a big white plastic sack. After a while, we all started to get hungry. Back then the food on the airplanes was not good at all. Dad reached for the plastic sack and began to pull out fresh Italian bread, Romano cheese and olives. The aroma immediately spread through the plane. Everybody was looking at us. The bread smelled so good. One stewardess kept walking by and staring at the bread. She did this several times and finally she asked, 'Can I have some?'"*

Food is so important in our special way of life. Jesus' last event before Crucifixion was at the table, breaking the bread. Much of life's enjoyment is around the table, so food is sacred. It is in the family where everybody comes together, to "gather" at the supper table. It is where the stories about your world news take place. What happened in the world of your family that day? But why would you want to gather around the table, to eat crummy food? Many people today do not cook, and/or they eat bland, tasteless, loveless food. There is no joy in that. There is joy in eating something good, joy in sharing good food.

Part III — Rising

Step 1 Prep:

a. Fill a large metal mixing bowl with hot water while making the dough

b. Have Wesson oil nearby.

Step 1 – The First Rise

a. Take the dough and put it into a large, **warm** metal bowl.

b. Pour a little Wesson oil in your hand and rub it over the top of the dough, coating the dough on all sides with the oil to keep it moist.

c. Place a large clear garbage bag on the dough. Cover the bowl completely, but leave the bag loose enough so that as the dough rises, the bag will go up with it, and will still cover the dough without restricting the rise.

d. Place the bowl in a warm spot (on the stove top with the oven on and door cracked).

e. Let the dough rise. The rise in the picture above spilled out over the pan before we got back to check it!

<u>Important:</u> *Keep warm the house, kitchen, or area the dough is rising in. In the winter, we keep it near the fireplace or open the oven door, with the oven on low heat, and place the dough on the door, spinning it every now and then to keep it evenly warm*

Step 2 – The Second Rise

a. When the dough has doubled and tripled in size, or is overflowing, knead the dough to get out the air. Notice how small, after kneading, the batch is.

b. Return the dough to a warm spot and let it rise again.

c. When the second full rise is achieved, knead again. This will be your second kneading. The dough is then ready to be divided and placed in your baking pans.

Step 3 Prep: Egg Mixture

This egg mixture will coat the top of the loaves. You will need the following:

- (8) eggs
- (2) tsp./10 mL water
- (2) Tbs./30 mL salted butter melted

d. Beat the eggs.

e. Add the water to the eggs.

f. While continuously stirring, add the melted butter to the mixture a little at a time, so the hot butter does not cook some of the eggs.

Step 3: The Baking Pan Rise

a. Coat the bottom of the bread pans with approximately ⅛ cup/30 mL of Wesson oil.

b. Using your hands, taking oil from the bottom, cover all the sides of the pan with oil. Oil should completely cover the side and bottom. Sometimes we put a little extra oil on the bottom to thicken the crust. You can experiment with this.

"When you fast, when I fast, your stomach tells you, 'I don't want to do that.' You say, 'You're going to do it.' Your stomach growls at you, like a dog wanting to bite you, 'Feed me. I'm hungry.' And you say, 'No. You are going to be subservient to my soul.'"

~Friend of Medjugorje

c. Drizzle a little of the egg mixture on the bottom of the pan if you want a really crispy, flavorful crust. But be careful, adding too much will make the crust soft. If this happens, you can put the bread back in the oven upside down with the upper element on to brown the bottom and help "crust it up."

"Through fasting, we move God to bind satan. God is very sensitive to a heart that denies their own hunger because of the love for Him. So God reciprocates by granting graces to kill satan's plans or his hold on us."

~ Friend of Medjugorje

d. Add dough to the pans. The amount of dough is important. The dough should have room to expand and rise. When it rises above the pan, it is time to bake.

e. Place pans in a warm spot to rise for about another hour or more as necessary.

f. If next to a heat source such as an oven, remember to turn the pans periodically so the dough is evenly heated. Of course, this is not necessary if your room is warm.

g. Let the dough rise until it comes to the top or just over the pan. Remember, you will get an oven rise also, so do not let the dough spill over the sides.

h. Just before going in the oven, very gently lift the dough, so as not to make the bread fall, and coat the top and sides of the dough liberally with the egg mixture. Fully cover the top of the bread with the egg mixture. We find ourselves often having to make another batch of egg mixture to cover all the loaves.

Colafrancesco's Italian Bread Recipe

During a nine-day fast, one of our joys is coming together to make bread. The smell of fresh bread baking in our large open **oven** fills the kitchen and hallways. A Friend of Medjugorje has always said that Our Lady's messages can be applied to <u>every</u> facet of daily life. We see this in our Community daily. Our Lady said on July 25, 2005, **"…Do n<u>oven</u>as of fasting and renunciation so that satan be far from you and grace be around you…"**

Part IV — Baking Small & Large Loaves

Step 1: Pre-heat oven to 450°F / 232°C

   a. Place the bread in the oven and bake at 450°F / 232°C for 10 minutes, then turn down the oven to 375°F / 190°C and continue to bake for 25 minutes or longer. Use your judgment, according to how your oven cooks. If using an electric oven, when setting the temperature, you can pour ¼ cup/60 mL of water in the bottom of the oven to add moisture, and quickly shut the door. If using a gas oven, spray some water into the oven.

If the bread is getting brown too quickly and not getting done in the center, you may turn the temperature down further. If the center is done and the bread is not a golden brown, turn the temperature down and bake a little longer. Remember, as already stated, the temperatures and times above are only guides, as every oven cooks differently.

    This bread is made through love and requires you to make it from beginning to end by "feel," meaning not only by physical touch but by your senses. This means tasting the dough at the different steps. Cook the bread to taste, not just by the recipe. From one batch to the next, you may have to adjust amounts of ingredients and times. The more you make it, the more you will learn. While this all may seem like alot of detail, it actually is not. It must be explained in detail for you to learn the style of how to make and bake Colafrancesco's Italian Bread. Once you've learned to do it by feel, it actually becomes easy and very gratifying to bake.

You can use different sized pans. These shown on page 122, are small terracotta pans from "Nature's Oven by Reco."* We use these "small loaf" pans when we want more of a crust per bite of bread. The large metal pans are from Williams Sonoma.** Notice in the picture on page 126, some of the loaves are light golden brown, and some are a little too browned. You have to monitor the bread carefully. To use smaller loaf pans, like the terracotta, adjust your baking time down. Our standard bread pans are 5"× 9", 1 pound metal loaf pans from Williams Sonoma.

Part V — Enjoy Your Homemade Bread!

Your kitchen should now be filled with the smell of homemade bread. Grab some butter and enjoy the richness of your labor. Be sure to share a loaf with your neighbor, even if you don't know them that well…and see what happens.

---

* Natures Oven By Reco Mini Bread Baker (Set of 4). You can order through Amazon.com

**Williams Sonoma 1 lb loaf metal pan. Can order online or in store.

Bread is Sacred

Many years ago, after throwing some bread in the garbage at our cabin in Medjugorje, a Friend of Medjugorje's wife witnessed one of their Croatian friends take the bread from the garbage and begin to eat it. Shocked, his wife asked the woman, whose name was Iva, what she was doing. She replied, "Bread is sacred." In Medjugorje, bread is held as sacred because Jesus chose to remain with us in this form. As a tradition, bread is never thrown in the garbage, rather, it is thrown into the yard to become food for birds and other creatures.

A Friend of Medjugorje and his brother share a profound childhood memory.

"Monsignor Keys, a tall Irish priest at our church, who we took bread to, once said, **"Bread is not meant to be cut, it's meant to be broken."** It struck us, and I understood it was because Jesus broke bread. *'He took bread, blessed it, broke it, and gave it to His disciples…'*"

Want more than just sliced bread?

During a nine-day bread and water fast, it's nice to have a little variety. A Friend of Medjugorje and his family have developed a few personal "favorites"—options for Colafrancesco's Italian Bread dough.

Fried Dough—The dough is made very thin and flat by hand or rolling pin, then fried in a skillet in plenty of olive oil. Be sure to make some holes in your flat dough, which will create a little crust at the edge of the hole, if you fry it right.

Small Loaves—These are "personal loaves" and are at a size that's easy to grab and go.

Rolls—Typically these rolls are made by separating the dough into balls and baking them in a round metal pan. Bake at 450°F / 232°C for 10 minutes, then turn down the oven to 375°F / 190°C for approximately 15 minutes more.

Fried Bread Bites—Fill a skillet with Wesson oil or olive oil (they cook differently, test it yourself and heat). Drop pieces of dough in the hot oil. The dough will expand and brown when ready. Take the bread out and put slices of butter, salt, cayenne pepper, etc., to taste.

Bread Crumbs—Save all stale bread. Let it harden on the counter. Grate into bread crumbs and use in meatballs, or breading for meat, fish, etc.

Colafrancesco's Italian Bread Recipe

Fasting: A Strong Foundation

A Friend of Medjugorje states:

"What parents embrace as a way of life, sets the foundation for their children's future way of life. Many parents teach their children to brush their teeth, go to bed early, go to school. They take them to the doctor when they are sick, and teach them about the practical things of everyday life. But they are crippling their children when they are only shown to put priority on material things, and no importance on virtues that lead to eternal life. Parents must, by their witness, show children how to acquire virtues, and Godly habits. If you let your <u>children</u> sleep in all the time, they will struggle the rest of <u>their</u> lives, crippled by not being an early riser. You witness to them to be an early riser by your own life, and this virtue will help them the rest of <u>their</u> lives to get to work, of which man has to do, as it was ordained by God in Genesis. Fasting is the same. You can imprint this in your children's spiritual DNA, by your fasting, by your love to do so, and by your love of bread! Thereby, fasting gives strength that will carry them through this life and into the next and enable them to help others to do the same."

Amazing. Amazing. Amazingly, there is only one food that will be eaten by every creature in the world, be it a snake, gorilla, insect, microbe, or dog. This one food is ordained by God Almighty, and is cored into every living creature by God. It is bread! The Bible says there are known realities in nature that prove the existence of God. How could this be by chance, except He foresaw what His own body would feed through the Eucharist! Bread, the Bread of all life. Our Lady of Medjugorje says, **"…Go into nature because there you will meet God, the Creator…"** This series of pictures unfolded in real time one Sunday during Rosary in the Field. Little Isabella loves her Italian bread, but so does the great dog named Rebel. She knows from experience to hold it where he can't get it. He waits until Isabella lowers her hand for a second and then snatches the bread from her hand. Tears and a shout of indignation burst forth as she holds onto the small piece of bread that is left and runs for safety. Rebel lingers longingly for one more bite, while Isabella is determined he not get her last piece of bread. ~ Friend of Medjugorje

#1 NATIONAL BESTSELLER
Over One Million Copies

Patriotic Rosary

For the Consecration of Our Nation
by a Friend of Medjugorje

Prayed in the Pentagon, convents, and every major patriotic event. A must-have for the Fourth of July, Veteran's Day, Memorial Day, and any other patriotic days.

A NEW BOOK BY A FRIEND OF MEDJUGORJE

What wonders await those who long to know more of the hidden life of the Holy Family. Our Lady lived half of Her life with St. Joseph, yet there is so little known of this humble, hidden man. Is that about to change? A Friend of Medjugorje sets the stage for incredible revelations that will soon be revealed to the world regarding St. Joseph.

See order form in the back of the book to order.

MEDJUGORJE
AND
THE MYSTERIES OF
SAINT
Joseph

The Newest Book by a Friend of Medjugorje That Will Shock and Stun You